To wildlife everywhere. May you always have a safe path to travel. – Billie

Für Papa. – Anke

© Text Billie Rooney 2025
© Illustrations Anke Noack 2025

All rights reserved. Except under the conditions described in the *Australian Copyright Act 1968* and subsequent amendments, no part of this publication may be reproduced, stored in a retrieval system or transmitted in any form or by any means, electronic, mechanical, photocopying, recording, duplicating or otherwise, without the prior permission of the copyright owner. Contact CSIRO Publishing for all permission requests.

Billie Rooney and Anke Noack assert their right to be known as the author or illustrator, respectively, of this work.

A catalogue record for this book is available from the National Library of Australia

ISBN: 9781486318100 (hbk)
ISBN: 9781486318117 (epdf)
ISBN: 9781486318124 (epub)

Published by:
CSIRO Publishing
36 Gardiner Road, Clayton VIC 3168
Private Bag 10, Clayton South VIC 3169
Australia

Telephone: +61 3 9545 8400
Email: publishing.sales@csiro.au
Website: www.publish.csiro.au
Sign up to our email alerts: publish.csiro.au/earlyalert

Edited by Belinda Bolliger
Cover artwork and concept design by Anke Noack
Text and cover design and layout by Samantha Metcalfe
Printed in China by Toppan Leefung Printing Limited

The views expressed in this publication are those of the author and illustrator and do not necessarily represent those of, and should not be attributed to, the publisher or CSIRO.

CSIRO acknowledges the Traditional Owners of the lands that we live and work on across Australia and pays its respect to Elders past and present. CSIRO recognises that Aboriginal and Torres Strait Islander peoples have made and will continue to make extraordinary contributions to all aspects of Australian life including culture, economy and science. CSIRO is committed to reconciliation and demonstrating respect for Indigenous knowledge and science. The use of Western science in this publication should not be interpreted as diminishing the knowledge of plants, animals and environment from Indigenous ecological knowledge systems.

Note for readers: A glossary can be found at the back of the book.

Note for teachers: Teacher notes are available at: https://www.publish.csiro.au/book/8147/#forteachers

Thank you to Gary Howling and Tandi Spencer-Smith from Great Eastern Ranges for their review of the manuscript.

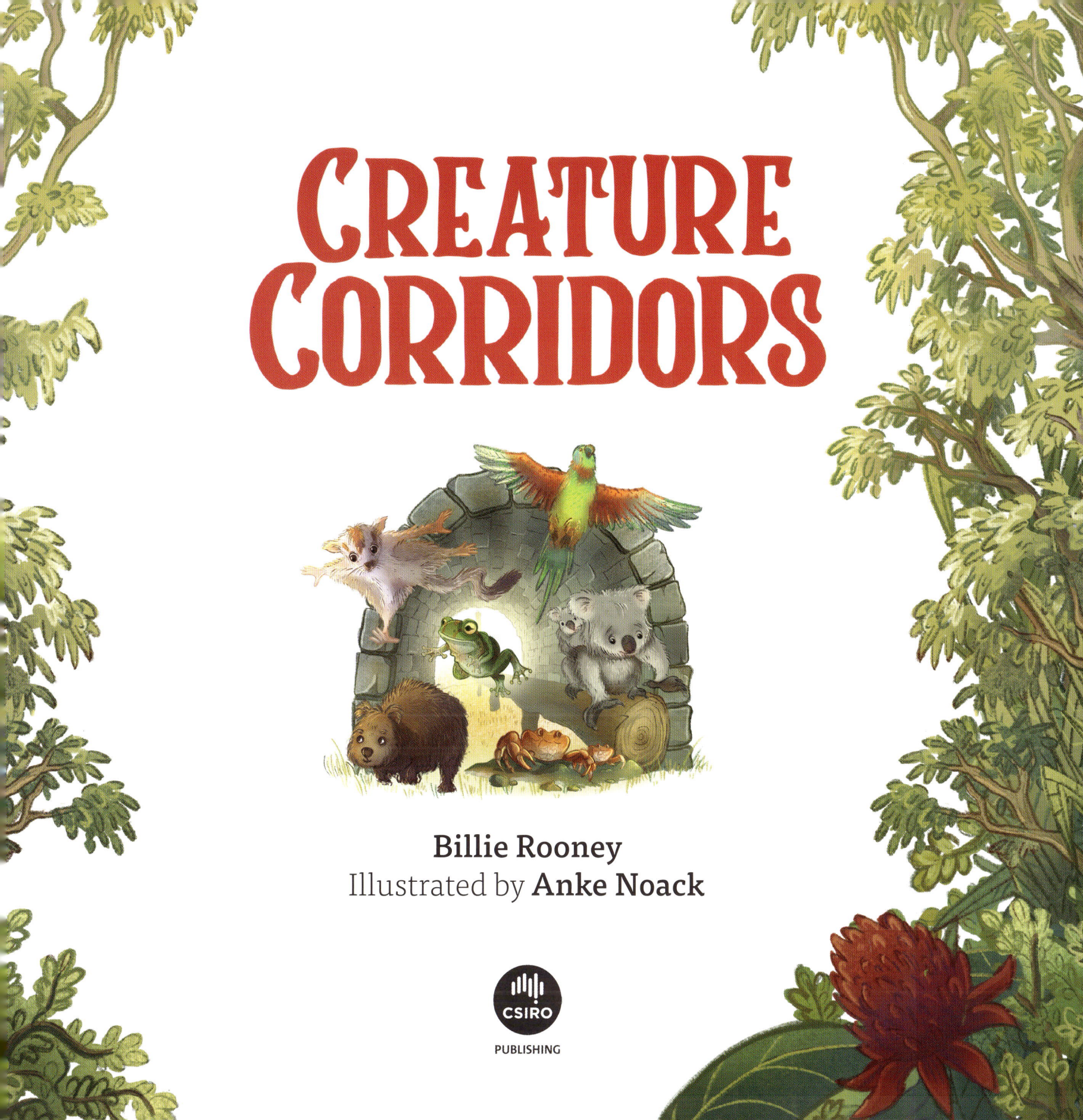

CREATURE CORRIDORS

Billie Rooney
Illustrated by Anke Noack

CSIRO PUBLISHING

We share the world with many creatures.

Some move by day,
others by night.
Some travel far and wide,
others stay closer to home.

Crawling, hopping, climbing or flying, wild creatures are on the move.

They search rivers and bush for food and water, places to breed and spaces to stay.

In this world we share with many creatures,
we have built
farms and factories,
hotels and highways,
dams and ditches
and streets that stretch into suburbs.

Food and shelter are hard to find.
There are many dangers.

To move safely, creatures need corridors.

Not corridors you find in schools or hospitals, but paths or patches of bush that make it safe to travel from here to there.

Wildlife corridors.

In a town bustling with cars and buses,
kangaroos thump, thump,

as if to say,
'This road is too dangerous.
How can we cross to the other side?'

A dusty path guides the kangaroos down a tunnel under the road, away from the cars.

A safe path to the grasslands.

On a farm cleared for crops,
birds tweet, tweet,
as if to say, 'Our trees have gone.
Where can we lay our eggs?'

They follow the scent of native nectar and spy a long row of trees leading to a clump of dense bushes.

A safe place to nest.

Near a highway rumbling with trucks and road trains,

koalas grunt, grunt,
as the air fills with stinky fumes.
Fresh gum trees seem far away.

The koalas find a bridge
built just for them
and soon work out how to use it.

A safe place to cross.

Along a mountain river,
platypus snuffle, snuffle,
as a water pump sucks the river dry
and the bank is cleared of trees.

The platypus find a stream that has been left to flow free and where trees and bushes shade the water.

A safe place for a burrow.

In a rainforest in northern Australia, cassowaries boom, boom, as if to say, 'Where can we find fruit now the trees are cut down?'

People plant new trees and pull down fences. Small forests join into one big forest and cassowaries can travel longer distances.

A safe path for finding food.

On an island in the Indian Ocean,
red crabs scuttle, scuttle,
as new rain says it's time to lay eggs.
Crabs scurry from the forest.

Some climb a metal bridge that takes them to the beach.
Others use roads that are closed to cars.

A safe path to the sea.

In a city backyard,
lizards scamper, scamper,
to keep away from dogs and cats
and foxes on the prowl.

The world we share with many creatures can be safe for us all.

WILDLIFE CORRIDORS

Animals need to move between different areas to find food, shelter or a place to breed. In many places, the pathways that animals travel along have become more dangerous. Some have been blocked altogether.

This is due to the construction of roads, buildings, fences, dams and other structures, as well as land that has been cleared. It means native animals now face more traffic on their pathways and have fewer trees and shrubs for protection. Predators such as dogs, cats and foxes can survive more easily in this new landscape and are also a threat to native animals.

Wildlife corridors provide safe pathways that animals can move along more freely. Corridors can include patches of bush, strips of vegetation alongside roads, or tree-lined rivers and streams that link protected areas of natural habitat. They can be as small as a backyard, the size of a park, or they can stretch across the country, linking forests and bush, rivers and seas.

We can help animals survive as they move around towns, cities and the countryside by making sure there are plenty of leafy corridors. These corridors need different types of trees, shrubs and grasses – tall and small, bushy and spiky – so that all kinds of animals can move around safely and find the food they need to eat.

Fallen branches or leaf litter on the ground provide safe places for creatures to burrow and feed, so it's best to leave these where they are. However, weeds and pests need to be managed as they can take over and destroy animal habitats.

Wildlife corridors were once everywhere. To make places safe for animals again, the corridors that have disappeared can be rebuilt. This can be done by looking for patches of habitat or bushland that are separated by a road or cleared land and then linking them back together by planting more vegetation. Wildlife corridors that already exist can be saved by planning ahead when new roads and houses are built.

This story shares a few types of wildlife corridors, but there are also many more.

CORRIDORS IN THE STORY

Kangaroos and towns

In many places in Australia, kangaroos live in bushland on the edge of town. They seek out grass to graze, roaming the streets and crossing roads on their way. Kangaroos are in danger of being hit by cars, especially during the early morning and evening when they are most active. Building tunnels under the roads can stop kangaroos from crossing where it is unsafe. Providing a dry path through the tunnel and planting vegetation right up to the entrance helps to guide kangaroos into the tunnels. New technologies can also help, such as virtual fences, which are poles placed by the side of the road that make a sound when a car is coming. The sound warns the animal not to cross.

Birds and farms

Lots of bushland is destroyed when it is cleared for crops such as wheat or cotton, or for grazing animals such as cows and sheep. Small native birds that can only fly short distances need trees and bushes for shelter, food and nesting places. Leaving patches of bush when clearing the land or planting rows of trees and shrubs between paddocks can help birds travel safely from place to place. Keeping old trees dotted across the paddocks is also important. These trees have hollows that provide homes for bigger birds and other animals in which to rest, shelter and breed.

Koalas and highways

Highways connect big towns and cities. They are used by cars, motorcycles, trucks and road trains. One way to help animals cross these busy roads is to build wildlife bridges. These are metal and concrete structures covered in trees and bushes that are similar to the surrounding wildlife habitat. Other bridges are made with rope ladders that extend over the road. By following the plants they are familiar with, animals learn where the bridges are and use these as corridors. These corridors are helpful for koalas, gliders, emus, wombats and many other animals.

Platypus, other water creatures and rivers

Wildlife corridors are also important in waterways. Our rivers and streams provide habitats and food for platypus and other creatures such as fish and turtles. Water levels in rivers can drop when they are used for irrigation or when dams are built. This can change the watery path that platypus and other creatures need so they can move upstream and downstream to find food and places to live and breed. For example, some fish need slower-moving water with logs and mud to hide in, while others need the water to flow strong and clear. Some fish must make the journey from the river to the sea and back again to breed. A healthy river can have all of these things if it is left to flow freely and if trees and bushes on the banks are protected.

Cassowaries and forests

Some forests have become smaller because the trees have been cut down to use for wood or land has been cleared to build new homes. People who want to look after our forests and the birds and other animals that live there are working to patch the forests back together. They plant new habitats to connect the forest that is left with nearby bushland and to make sure there are lots of stops along the way for creatures such as cassowaries. The southern cassowary is one of the world's largest birds. It lives in Queensland and eats fruits from the rainforest and other nearby forests. It is an important species that helps to spread seeds and keep the rainforest growing. Connecting the forests back together provides a larger area for the cassowary to move around.

Crabs and the sea

Each year on Christmas Island, millions of red crabs come out of the forest and head to the sea to breed. To get safely to the sea, they have to cross roads. Special bridges have been built to help them do this. During the crabs' migration time, cars are not allowed on some roads. The female red crab can produce up to 100,000 eggs. She waits in a burrow in the sand for the eggs to develop and then releases them into the sea where they hatch into tiny red crabs. Once the baby crabs are big enough (about 5 millimetres across), they head back to the forest. The crabs also have predators in the sea, such as rays and sharks. Having a special red crab corridor between the sea and the forest helps to make sure many will still survive.

Lizards and backyards

Ensuring safe places for animals can start in your backyard, school playground or local park. Planting small patches of native bushes and trees gives shelter to animals as they travel through a city or town. Flowers provide food for birds, butterflies and bees. Trees provide homes for bats, birds and possums. A birdbath or pond collects water for frogs, birds and lizards. Having safe spots up high, keeping cats in enclosed spaces and inside at night, and being a responsible dog owner helps many little creatures stay safe from predators.

If we plant small leafy areas in backyards, schools or parks, these will join up to become long green strips that make perfect wildlife corridors. When these green places have a variety of plants and other materials such as rocks and logs, they provide the best wildlife corridor of all.

GLOSSARY

Breed: How animals produce their young.

Bushland: Land that has not been cleared for housing or other development and is covered in trees, shrubs and grasses.

Fumes: The gas that comes from a car or truck engine, which can be dangerous if breathed in large amounts.

Grassland: Land that is open and covered mainly in grasses, with only a few trees.

Habitat: The place where an animal lives. It provides everything that the animal needs to survive, including food, water and shelter.

Irrigation: Pumping water from rivers and streams to water crops and orchards.

Nectar: The sugary liquid produced by flowers.

Predator: An animal that hunts, kills and eats other animals.

Protected areas: Land that is protected by law from development because it is important for plants and animals.

Rainforest: A forest with many tall trees that grows where there is lots of rain and the climate is warm.

Species: A group of animals with similar features and related in a way that means they can breed with each other.

Vegetation: All the plant life covering a particular area, including trees, shrubs, flowers and grasses.

Wildlife corridor: A stretch of land or water that connects animal habitats so that creatures can safely move in search of food, water, places to shelter and breeding partners.